P ATH B L A Z E R S

*Eight People Who Made
a Difference*

*P*ATHBLAZERS

EIGHT
PEOPLE
WHO MADE
A DIFFERENCE

by M. K. FULLEN

Illustrated by SELMA WALDMAN

OPEN HAND PUBLISHING INC.

Seattle, Washington

OPEN HAND PUBLISHING INC.

P.O. Box 22048, Seattle, Washington 98122

(206)447-0597

Distributed by **The Talman Company, Inc.**

150 Fifth Avenue, New York, NY 10011

(212)620-3182 • (212)627-4682 FAX

Book and cover design:

Deb Figen • ART & DESIGN SERVICES • Seattle, Washington

Cover Illustration:
Septima Clark by Selma Waldman

Library of Congress Cataloging-in-Publication Data

Fullen, M. K., 1954-
    Pathblazers : eight people who made a difference : a
collection of short biographies / by M. K. Fullen ; illustrations by
Selma Waldman. -- 1st ed.
        p.   cm.
    Includes bibliographic references (p.).
    Contents: Septima Clark — Jester Hairston — Josephine Baker —
Gwendolyn Brooks — Thurgood Marshall — James Forman — Andrew
Young — Barbara Jordan.
    ISBN 0-940880-35-0 (cloth cover) : $12.95 — ISBN 0-940880-36-9
(paperback) : $6.95
    1. Afro-Americans—Biography—Juvenile literature. [1. Afro
-Americans—Biography.] I. Waldman, Selma, 1938- ill.
II. Title.
E185.96.F85 1992
920'.009296'073--dc20
[B]   91-46484
                                                              CIP
                                                              AC

FIRST EDITION

Printed in the United States of America
96 95 94 93 92   8 7 6 5 4 3 2 1

To my four Pathblazers,
for making a way
out of no way ...
Richard, Leola, Darrell, and Nickolas.

M. K. F.

To the memory of Vincent J. Davis (1910 - 1990)
who blazed a path of community and generosity,
speaking the truth to all those who were treated
to the expansiveness of his friendship.

S. W.

Contents

In the citizenship school,
Septima taught people not to be afraid.

S E P T I M A C L A R K

1898 – 1987

The freezing wind slapped the tiny log cabin again and again. Inside, a handful of schoolchildren huddled around the big stone fireplace trying to keep warm.

"Isaiah, I hate to ask this of you, but would you please fetch more firewood?" Isaiah looked up at his teacher, Miss Clark, then glanced out of the window at the waves smashing against the shore.

"Is it my turn, Miss Clark?" Isaiah asked woefully. Septima Clark turned slightly and laid a soft hand on Isaiah's shoulder.

"Yes honey, it's your turn." She smiled at his upturned face. Isaiah gathered his thin coat around him and headed for the door. As he opened it, the wind barreled in, nipping at the other children's hands and feet.

"All right children, let's continue with our lesson. Frederick Douglass was a great man. Why?" asked Miss Clark of her young students. Ruth raised her hand. "Because he fought for the rights of our people."

"Very good, Ruth," said Miss Clark, clapping her hands with praise. "Let's continue."

Isaiah returned with an armful of wood, laid it on the hearth and everyone started to warm up.

At the end of the day the children bundled up for the cold walk home. Stuffing their homework assignments into coat pockets, they left the cabin. Miss Clark swept up her classroom, erased the blackboard and emptied the ashes from the fireplace. Then she prepared to go home too. She carefully wrapped her brown woolen scarf around her ears and pulled on her winter coat. She wrapped rags and newspaper over her boots as extra protection against frostbite. Now she was ready for the walk home.

Septima Clark had lots to think about during her four-mile walk. "I call it my pondering time," she used to say. She often thought about the African-American people on Johns Island where she lived.

Johns Island was part of a cluster of islands around the harbor of Charleston, South Carolina. You could only reach the island by boat. The people who lived there worked the land, and the only food they had was what they grew. For this reason, children often missed school because they needed to help on the farm.

This disturbed Miss Clark. She knew that the children needed an education so that when they grew up they would not be as poor as their parents. But how? How could the children and parents of Johns Island come to see how important school was?

Miss Clark continued her walk past the gloomy, muddy swamp toward the rooming house where she lived. As she climbed the stairs an idea came to her! "If the children can't come to school, I'll bring it to them!

I'll start a school for anyone who wants to learn. I'll teach everyone to read. The elders, the mamas, daddies and everyone! And they'll learn from their own experience."

That night, by the glow of a kerosene lamp, Septima Clark made up whimsical stories about sea birds, island animals and swamp creatures. As dawn was splitting the water's edge, Septima stretched and smiled. "I'll ask Esau Jenkins to help me." Esau had grown up on Johns Island and he was more than willing to help. Some white people on the island didn't want Black folks to learn how to read and write, so Septima and Esau hid their school for adults behind a grocery store.

Soon the school was overflowing with people. Miss Clark taught children in the daytime and adults at night.

"Many grownups wanted to learn to read so they could vote. This was their goal," said Septima. When a person in South Carolina went to register to vote, they had to read the laws about voting and parts of the Constitution out loud. If they could not read, they could not vote.

Septima decided she needed more education herself. She had heard of the Highlander Folk School in Tennessee. Highlander's purpose was to bring people of all races together to figure out how to fight racism nonviolently. Septima felt the only way things could improve for African-Americans was if they voted and became involved in the process of elections.

During her time of study at Highlander, Septima was fired from her teaching position on Johns Island because she was a member of the National Association for the Advancement of Colored People (NAACP). When the people at Highlander found out that she had lost her job, they offered her a job as director of workshops for the school.

Septima journeyed all over the South setting up Citizenship Schools so people could learn to read and vote. Septima's job was to teach people not to be afraid. She also trained other people how to teach, and more and more Black people learned to read and vote. In the 1960's, Septima's Citizenship Schools served as a model for the Freedom Schools set up by Civil Rights activists.

Years later, Septima rested in her rocking chair. A tiny amber-colored woman, she was called the "Mother of the Civil Rights Movement." She still wore her hair in six tight plaits around her head. It looked like a crown. Her chair made a soft creaking sound as she rocked.

"I just want all people to stand up straight and tall and fight for their rights."

Septima Clark died December 15, 1987, on her beloved Johns Island, South Carolina.

Jester raises his baton and says,
"Make the people proud; honor the ancestors!"

JESTER HAIRSTON

1902 - present

"Jester, Jester, please go fetch me some water."

"Ah, Granny, do I have to?" Jester whined and kicked the dust on the dirt road that ran by the house.

"Yes, Jester, you have to. I need water now if I'm going to fix supper."

"But Granny, you know who lives over by the creek." He raised a pitiful glance in Granny's direction.

Granny wouldn't change her mind but she promised, "Now, everyone knows the ghosts only come out at night. Go on with you and fetch me that water." Cautiously, Jester made his way down the winding path toward the freshwater creek nearby. The low hanging trees drew long, dark shadows across his feet as he walked. Creeping toward the water's edge, his eyes darted in every direction at every sound his ears picked up. A twig broke and bushes rustled. He was scared. Everyone believed the ghosts of dead slaves roamed the area encircling the creek.

Granny and all of her friends gathered at the house on hot, lazy Sunday afternoons and remembered slavery times. Aunt Minn would say, "Berthe, do you remember when Massa Tom sold Lizzy away from Big Jim? He was begging and pleading to keep her, but Massa Tom wanted to make an example out of them. He had to prove that slaves weren't really married, not legally anyhow."

"And do you remember," Berthe would say, "when Nat Turner and his boys planned that wonderful escape and freed up a whole lot of plantations before they got caught?"

"Berthe, do you recall Harriet Tubman," Minn would respond, "took all those folks to freedom."

Jester lay on his back in the sweet-smelling grass and listened as hard as he could to those stories. Then the idea came to him! He would tell the slaves' stories, so no one would ever forget! But how? How could he get people to really listen to the tales? He had it! People will always listen to music.

Jester decided to prepare himself for a career in music. This was a giant task, but he was ready to meet the challenge. "No matter what I have to go through to get my education, I will! The slave stories are history! I can't let people forget what the slaves lived through."

Jester studied hard through high school. His work was rewarded when he was admitted to Tufts University in Boston. Jester was one of the first African-American students to be admitted to Tufts.

Jester lived in a meager little room near the campus. He turned his kitchen table into a desk and spent countless hours studying endless pages of music. He didn't have a piano in his room, so he practiced by tapping his fingers on the table top, according to the notes on the sheet music. "I won't be satisfied until I memorize this score."

After graduation, Jester journeyed to New York for further study. He was accepted at the Julliard School of Music. "I can learn to be a concert singer here." But even as he trained, the slave songs still danced in Jester's ears.

While wandering the streets of New York one day, Jester heard the songs of his childhood coming from an old rehearsal hall. Jester followed the music up a dark, creaky staircase. He pushed open the door and was greeted by a hundred singers harmonizing, "Get On Board Little Children." Jester auditioned on the spot and was accepted into the Hall Johnson Choir. Before long, Jester became the assistant conductor of the choir.

The Hall Johnson Choir performed as singers and chorus members in Broadway shows. Hall and Jester wove slave songs into every corner of their act. The melodies spoke of slavery and of chopping cotton and cutting cane in the fields. There were also gentle lullabies. Some slave songs even preached about escape. During slavery times, the masters and overseers had no idea that the work songs the slaves were singing had hidden meanings.

Although everyone in the choir had an excellent voice, Jester's stood out. Soon he was asked to perform in other shows and on the radio. Hollywood called, and Jester moved to the West Coast. "No matter what I do, I'll sing the songs of my people," he said. Producers and casting directors started to ask him to write music for movies. Then they discovered this man was a bundle of talent! Jester could act too! He appeared in *Porgy and Bess, To Kill a Mockingbird, In The Heat of the Night* and dozens more movies. He also wrote and performed the song "Amen" in the movie *Lilies of the Field.*

This sable-colored man with the wide smile and laughing eyes continued to teach the world slave songs. In 1961, the United States State Department appointed Jester Goodwill Ambassador. This special post enabled him to travel and teach choirs all over the world to sing slave songs. When Jester strolls out on an empty stage, he raises his baton and says, "Make the people proud, honor the ancestors!" With that, the performing hall erupts with the voices of a Swedish, Finnish, Nigerian or Chinese choir singing the words of a once-enslaved people.

Today, Jester continues to travel the world, sharing the heritage of African-Americans in song. He has received fifty honorary doctorate degrees from universities throughout the country. Now ninety years old, Jester appears regularly in the television show, *Amen.* He is considered an expert on African-American folk music. Jester says, "I'm just a storyteller. Everyone has a story to share."

Josephine, the most sought-after entertainer in Europe, adopted orphaned children and raised them as her "Rainbow Tribe."

JOSEPHINE BAKER

1906 - 1975

"**Come one, come all!** See the great Josephine dance and sing for you! See her as you've never seen her before! Only a penny a ticket, one red cent!"

Josephine stood on the top step of the shabby front porch. She was yelling at the top of her lungs, waving her skinny chestnut-colored arms and nearly freezing in the cold winter weather. But she continued to call the kids in the neighborhood.

"Just a penny will buy you a seat at the show of shows! Miss Josephine will prance and sparkle across the stage, dazzling you with moves you've never seen before!"

As the kids came up the steps, she collected their pennies and ushered them into a tiny corner of the living room where she had set up a stage. Her mama and papa were at work and didn't know that she used the tattered blue living room curtains as her dancing costume.

Josephine and her family lived in St. Louis, Missouri. The family was very poor. During the long, cold winters, Josephine's father made the children's winter boots out of cardboard boxes. Mama, Papa and all of the children had to work just so they could eat. Mama was always trying to figure out how to stretch a meal. Sometimes Josephine and her sister Margaret would go through the neighbors' garbage cans looking for scraps of meat to put in their mother's soup for dinner.

Josephine began working when she was only seven years old. She lied about her age and when she wasn't singing and dancing, she picked up odd jobs in the neighborhood. She would clean and wax floors, haul coal for heat, anything to make a few extra quarters. But she loved to sing and dance best of all.

Sometimes Josephine and her sister Margaret would save enough money to go to the Booker T. Washington Theater. Black people were allowed to see the vaudeville acts on Saturday afternoons. The rest of the week the theater was reserved for white people only.

Since Saturday was the only day of the week they could attend, Josephine made sure she was first in line. One day the Dixie Steppers Dance Troupe came to town all the way from New York. They sang, danced and told rich, colorful stories. Josephine sat on the very edge of her seat gazing up at the dancers who performed magic with their feet. She decided she could do that too. Josephine knew she had to work and what better way to make money then by being in show business?

At the end of the show, Josephine jumped out of her seat and went backstage to find the director. Mustering up all of her courage, she asked, " Mister, please give me a job. I can sing and dance. I've got lots of experience. I'm really good." Josephine didn't tell him the only experience she'd had was on her homemade stage in the living room. She knew she could do it. He hired her on the spot.

She was officially in show business!

Soon it was time for the Dixie Steppers to leave St. Louis and tour the rest of the country. Josephine had to make a big decision. Would she go on the road, or stay in St. Louis? She could help support the family better on a dancer's salary than by picking up odd jobs. It was clear that she had to go. Josephine boarded the train with only the clothes on her back and one pair of shoes. No one knew she was only thirteen years old.

When they arrived in New York, Josephine was hypnotized by the sights and sounds of the city. The streets were so busy and the buildings were so tall. She had made it to Broadway, the greatest theater district in the country! She danced and clowned nightly with the Dixie Steppers, and the audiences loved it.

A wealthy woman noticed Josephine and asked her if she would like to perform in France. Josephine gasped, "You mean where the Eiffel Tower is? I'd love to go."

Soon after, a group of twenty-five African-American singers, dancers and musicians boarded the ocean liner that would carry them to France. Josephine had never been on a boat before.

The troupe with which she performed in Paris was named the Revue Negre. Josephine loved everything about Paris. There the color of her skin wasn't a problem. She could eat in any restaurant and live in any neighborhood she chose. Josephine could not have done these things in the United States. Back home, Black people drank out of "colored only" drinking fountains and sat in the back of the bus or train. There were many places where they were not allowed to go. In Paris,

Josephine was treated just like anybody else. For the first time in her life, she felt FREE.

Josephine Baker became the most sought-after entertainer in Europe. She dressed in beautiful gowns decorated with sequins and feathers. She sang and danced in theaters all over the continent. She became rich and famous, but she wanted something more. Josephine wanted to stop racism.

World War II had broken out and Nazi soldiers marched into Paris. The Nazi party was based on racism. The Nazis believed that white people were superior and their plan was to eliminate all people who were not white. Josephine knew that Nazi racism was like the racism against her people in the United States, and she had to do something to stop it.

She became an undercover agent for the French Resistance. She traveled all over Europe and North Africa carrying sheet music containing messages written in invisible ink for the generals. The enemy never suspected her. They thought she was just a singer. After the war, Josephine was decorated with the Legion of Honor Medal for service to France. When she retired from the service, her rank was that of lieutenant.

During the war, Josephine saw much destruction and suffering. She knew how much the children suffered. Many, many children were injured and lost both of their parents. Josephine and her husband decided to adopt orphaned children from all over the world. They called their family the "Rainbow Tribe," and they demonstrated that people of different nationalities, different races and different religions could live together as brothers and sisters. They bought a castle that was nestled in the

French countryside. It even had its own zoo. The screeches of monkeys and the lullaby of exotic birds could be heard all over the estate.

Josephine continued performing and entertaining all over the world. When she visited the United States, she would sometimes disguise herself and travel to the South. This way she could hear the stories of her people. She often heard that their lives had been threatened simply because they wanted to vote or get better school facilities for their children.

Josephine made speeches against racism all over the country. She refused to perform in places where Black people and white people were not allowed to sit together. She worked constantly for change, to make the world a better place.

Josephine Baker performed until she was sixty-eight. One night, after a triumphant performance at the Follies Bergères in Paris, she died peacefully in her sleep.

Gwennie would sit on the
steps behind her house
and gaze at the sky.
She loved clouds.
What she saw
inspired her to
write poems.

GWENDOLYN BROOKS

1917 - present

I wonder if the elephant

Is lonely in his stall

When all the boys and girls are gone

And there's no shout at all,

And there's no one to stamp before,

No one to note his might.

Does he hunch up, as I do,

Against the dark of night?

Gwendolyn Brooks

"Did you know you can read your future in the clouds? That's right. If you stare at them long enough, you'll see your life dance across the sky."

Gwendolyn Brooks believed that. When she was a little mahogany-tinted girl with freshly pressed curls, Gwennie would sit on the cold stone steps behind her house in Chicago and gaze at the sky. She concentrated so hard on the clouds that words began to float into her head. She started to write them down. Her cloud-inspired words appeared as all kinds of poems.

As she got older, Gwendolyn realized two very important things: "One thing was that I am deliciously dark skinned. When I was young, I would thrust my arm out, right in front of me and study it. I'd look at the way light played off of it, making the color bright and polished. I loved it."

The second thing Gwendolyn realized was that she was not popular. But being popular was not as important to Gwendolyn as reading everything she could get her hands on. When Gwendolyn wasn't sitting in her window seat reading or sitting on the stone steps watching the clouds, she was writing. She wrote at least a poem a day and sometimes two or three. She kept big, fat notebooks of her poems.

At thirteen, Gwendolyn published her first poem in *American Childhood*. It was called "Eventide." At sixteen, she was a weekly contributor to the *Chicago Defender*, an African-American newspaper in Chicago. She had seventy-five poems published in the "Lights and Shadows" column in only two years.

Gwendolyn was always looking for ways to enhance her writing talents, so she began searching for a writing group. She enrolled in a class at the Southside Community Arts Center. Here she was surrounded by writers, painters, sculptors and other African-Americans dedicated to art.

"I was so excited to be in the company of people who were so talented," Gwendolyn said. "I knew some of them must be cloud gazers like me." As a result of these new friendships, Gwendolyn devoted even more time to her writing. She felt brave enough to start entering writing contests. When she won the Midwestern Writer's Conference Award, a book publisher called her.

"Miss Brooks, have you written enough poems for a book?"

"Have I ever!" was Gwendolyn's reply. This was how her first book, *A Street Called Bronzeville*, was born.

Gwendolyn spent hours and days at the library poring over research material. The more she learned about Africans and African-Americans, the more African-centered her work and her life became.

"Before I started looking around, no one had taught me my history. I didn't know that the slaves were the kings and queens of Africa. Or that Africa had the first university in the world. All people should know these things."

Gwendolyn wrote more books, poems and book reviews. She also began a teaching career. "I believe all students have something to say. They can paint pictures with words if someone shows them how."

Annie Allen was a book Gwendolyn wrote that explored the different attitudes in the Black community.

She wrote about rich Blacks, poor Blacks and those in between. None were able to escape the pain brought about by racism. This book won the Pulitzer Prize for Literature, the most valued award in American literature. Gwendolyn was the first African-American woman to receive this great honor.

Now people from all over the world were reading her work. Students were clamoring to get into her classes. Gwendolyn had never realized that she might become a famous person. "I just want to work in the community," Gwendolyn said.

There was a street gang in Chicago called the Blackstone Rangers. Many people were afraid of them, but not Gwendolyn. When she heard that some of the gang members had a secret wish to write, she said, "Well, bring them on!" Sitting in a circle with some of the Rangers, Gwendolyn said, "We come together to share our Africanness through our words, our stories and our plays. Everyone has a lot to say."

So many people loved Gwendolyn's poems and stories that she was made Poet Laureate for the state of Illinois. This honor meant the whole state recognized her talent. The Library of Congress in Washington, D.C. also knew what a great writer she was and invited her to become Poetry Consultant to the Library of Congress, one of the highest honors an American author can achieve. Gwendolyn was recognized as a national treasure.

Today, Gwendolyn still writes and teaches. She travels around the country giving readings in prisons, as well as in schools and universities. She lives in the same house she grew up in, and still studies the clouds.

*Supreme Court Justice Thurgood Marshall
fought for the constitutional rights of all Americans.*

THURGOOD MARSHALL

1908 — present

"Your great-granddaddy was so mean, his master freed him just to be rid of him."

While Thurgood Marshall was growing up, he heard lots of stories about his ornery great-grandfather, who had been a slave. In one story, Thoroughgood Marshall's master said to him, "I brought you here from Africa so I guess I can't very well shoot you—as you deserve. On the other hand, I can't in clear conscience sell anyone as vicious as you to another slaveholder. So I'm going to set you free, on the condition you get out of this county and never come back."

After he was freed, Thurgood's great-grandfather moved a few miles away, built a house and raised a family. He was mean, but he taught his children self-respect and dignity.

Thurgood Marshall's parents taught Thurgood these same values. But it was no longer possible to escape racism just by being mean. Thurgood was brought up to be respectful of all kinds of people, and also to be able to defend himself from anyone who was disrespectful of him.

Young Thurgood Marshall stood up in front of his fifth-grade class full of brown faces looking at him. Many of them grinned as he recited the 14th Amendment of the Constitution:

> "All persons born or naturalized in the United States, and subject to the jurisdiction thereof, are citizens of the United States and of the State wherein they reside. No State shall make or enforce any law which shall abridge the privileges of immunities of citizens of the United States; nor shall any State deprive any person of life, liberty, or property, without due process of law, nor deny to any person within its jurisdiction the equal protection of the laws."

Thurgood had to memorize these lines as punishment for fooling around in class, but they were words he would always remember. He would spend most of his life working to make them apply to all Americans.

Thurgood lived with his parents and his older brother in a racially mixed middle-class neighborhood in Baltimore, Maryland. His mother Norma was an elementary school teacher. His father Will was a dining-car waiter and a steward in a private club. Although Will Marshall had been too poor to get much education when he was young, he loved to read and write. He taught Thurgood how to win an argument by using logic and facts to prove his point. Will Marshall liked to follow court cases, and sometimes he took Thurgood with him to the courthouse to watch a trial take place.

Thurgood was a bright student but he also liked to have fun. He often got into trouble for playing pranks in class. Anybody who made trouble in class was banished to the basement of the school with a copy of the United States Constitution. Since Thurgood was frequently sent to the basement, he knew the entire Constitution by heart when he finished elementary school.

One evening Thurgood recited the 14th Amendment to his father and then he asked, "But if we're citizens of the United States, why can't I go to the school I want? And why can't I sit where I want to at the movies?"

"Son," Will Marshall replied, "I can't argue with you. All I can say is, the Constitution describes things as they ought to be, not as they are."

After Thurgood graduated from high school, his mother wanted him to become a dentist. Thurgood went to Lincoln University in Pennsylvania, but he wasn't sure what he wanted to do. During his first year in college he spent more time playing pranks than studying, but in his second year Thurgood settled down. Using what he had learned from his father about winning an argument, Thurgood discovered that he liked debating better than dentistry. One of his favorite topics was equal rights for African-Americans.

At Lincoln University, Thurgood met students from all over the United States, as well as from Africa and Asia. One crisp cold October night, Thurgood and some of his friends decided it was time for the theater in town to let African-Americans sit wherever they like. They disliked always having to sit in the balcony while whites sat in the plush seats in the orchestra section. After buying their tickets, Thurgood and his friends settled into a few of the empty seats at the front of the theater. As they watched the cowboy movie on the screen, an usher with a beaming flashlight approached the group. "Hey, you can't sit here!" he whispered loudly. Thurgood and his friends quietly ignored him and watched the movie. "I said you can't sit here!"

Thurgood glanced at the usher and whispered back, "We paid for our tickets and this is where we choose to sit." The usher walked away. From then on Thurgood and his friends sat where ever they wanted at the movie theater.

After graduating from Lincoln, Thurgood Marshall attended the School of Law at Howard University in Washington, D.C. He spent a lot of time in the library, researching legal questions. He worked closely with two of his teachers, Professor Charles Hamilton Houston and Professor William Henry Hastie. When Houston and Hastie met to discuss cases and practice their arguments, Thurgood joined in and was not afraid to challenge his teachers.

Professor Hastie was asked to be part of a very important legal team in the South in 1932, and he asked Thurgood to help him. A young Black man wanted to attend the University of North Carolina Law School. The school refused him entrance because he was Black. Since North Carolina had no law school for Blacks, the young man decided to sue the school. The state was supposed to provide "separate but equal" education for all. The young man hoped his suit would force the University to accept him.

Thurgood read law books until his eyes burned. "This young man has every right to attend the law school!" Professor Hastie said. "We have come up with the best arguments we can, and we are going to make history with this case!" Unfortunately they lost the case, but that only made Thurgood more determined to right what he saw was wrong.

Thurgood read law books until his eyes burned.

Charles Houston left Howard University to become the head of a branch of the National Association for the Advancement of Colored People (NAACP), a powerful organization that fights for people's rights. After Thurgood graduated from law school he was asked by Charles Houston to be a lawyer for the NAACP. Thurgood fought hard in the courts for the NAACP, using the Constitution as his weapon. He traveled all over the country to represent people who had experienced discrimination.

One of the cases that Thurgood and the NAACP took up was to change the course of American history. It is called *Brown v. The Board of Education of Topeka*. It had been ruled in Topeka, Kansas, that seven-year-old Linda Brown would not be allowed to attend the all-white school near her home. Instead, she had to cross dangerous train tracks to catch a bus to the "colored school." The Supreme Court of the United States agreed to listen to an appeal of this decision. For three days Thurgood Marshall argued the case before the Supreme Court.

It took more than a year for the Supreme Court to reach its decision. They finally ruled that segregation of schools in the United States is illegal. It had been a long, hard fight for Thurgood Marshall and the other lawyers of the NAACP, but the law was changed. The "separate but equal" law that had been in effect for fifty years, and that Thurgood Marshall had been fighting for twenty-five years, had been ended. "I was so happy, I was numb," he said later.

Making a new law was only the first step. Many schools refused to obey the order to integrate, so Thurgood Marshall was in the forefront of the struggle to make schools obey the Constitution. He gave Autherine Lucy support as they both stood in front of the

University of Alabama where she was insisting on her right to enroll. He traveled to Japan and Korea to help Black Americans who were being discriminated against in themilitary. Back in the United States, he argued in court and to the public for the right of African-American children to attend school in Little Rock, Arkansas.

When leaders of the African nation of Kenya were putting together a new government, they asked Thurgood Marshall to come help them write their constitution. Soon after Thurgood Marshall returned to the United States, President John Kennedy appointed him a judge in the Court of Appeals for the Second Circuit, one of eleven Circuit Courts in the federal court system. He was the first Black man to hold this powerful position. In 1961, President Lyndon Johnson appointed Thurgood Marshall Solicitor General of the United States. This is the third-highest legal position in the country. The Solicitor General represents the United States in front of the Supreme Court.

And then in 1967, President Johnson appointed Thurgood Marshall to become a judge on the Supreme Court, the highest court in the land. Justice Marshall was the first African-American to hold this position. From his seat on the Supreme Court, Thurgood Marshall continued to fight for the constitutional rights of all Americans for twenty-four years. He retired in 1991.

*James set the Coke back on the cooler and walked out
of the drugstore. He walked and walked,
thinking about what had happened*

JAMES FORMAN

1928— present

It was a long train ride from Chicago, where James was born, to Marshall County, Mississippi, where his grandmother lived. James had made the trip many times, but this time he was traveling alone. He looked forward to stopping over in Memphis to visit his auntie. He knew just how to find her house from the station.

When James got off the train, he was hit with a blast of southern summer heat. Folding his jacket carefully over his arm, James started down the street in search of something cool to drink. He knew he had better be the best-dressed, best-mannered six-year-old boy in Memphis, or he'd be in big trouble when he got to his auntie's house.

James strolled into a drugstore and climbed up on one of the plush leather stools. He was the only person in the shop. After a long time, a waitress approached him. She didn't smile.

"What do you want?" she said.

"May I please have a Coke and a glass?" James said. He already knew how good the cold Coke would taste sliding down his throat. The waitress left. After another long wait, a man appeared and asked James, "So you want a Coke?"

James smiled and said, "Yes, please."

The man told James to follow him. He took him around to the Coca-Cola cooler and pulled out a bottle. James said, "No. I want to drink it at the counter."

"Boy, Negroes don't sit at the counter."

James didn't fully understand the man's words, but he felt like all the wind had been knocked out of him. He set the Coke back on the cooler and walked out of the drugstore. James walked and walked, thinking about what had happened. He realized that there were things he could not do because he had brown skin. He couldn't even sit down and have a Coke.

James loved being on his grandmother's farm. The family was very poor but there were cousins to play with and aunts and uncles to look after him. James called his grandmother "Mama Jane" and she affection-ately called him "Spote," a country way of saying "Sport." James helped collect wood for the stove and fireplace and bring in water from the well in the backyard. In the summer there were fresh vegetables from the garden, but in the winter there wasn't enough food. Sometimes

James was so hungry that he ate dirt. But the family had each other. They tried to protect James from the hostile world that surrounded them.

Later that summer, James was playing in Mama Jane's house when there was a knock on the door. Mama Jane said, "Spote, you go answer the door." When James opened the door, he saw a man standing there who looked like a ghost. James ran to his grandmother. "Mama Jane, it's a man with a white face and I'm scared!"

"See what he wants," Mama Jane answered. James went back to the door as slowly as possible, hoping the man would be gone. He wasn't. "My grandma asked me to find out what you want," James said.

"Ask your Mama if she could give me some bread or something to eat," he said. James ran back to tell his grandmother. "He says he's hungry, Mama Jane. What should we do?"

"Well, go to the panty and get him some leftover cornbread." James did as he was told but was surprised. He didn't know that white folks got hungry, too. Learning that all people, no matter what race they are, can be poor and hungry was a lesson James would remember his entire life.

• • • • •

While Jim Forman was a student at the University of Southern California he decided to become a writer. He wanted to share his thoughts and the experiences of his life with the rest of the world. But one night as he was leaving the library, he was arrested by the police. They falsely accused him of committing a robbery. The police took him to jail. They beat him and would not allow him to telephone a lawyer or a friend for help. When James was finally released, his body hurt all over. He felt confused and angry. He decided to leave Los Angeles to try to heal from the brutal experience.

Jim went back to Chicago and attended Roosevelt University. In his senior year, he was elected president of the student council. All through college, he went on writing down his thoughts and experiences.

In 1958, Jim traveled to Little Rock, the capital of Arkansas, where Thurgood Marshall and others were working to integrate the public schools. The Supreme Court had ordered an end to segregation, and all of the public schools in Little Rock were closed. They stayed closed for an entire year. When the schools re-opened, people all over the world saw pictures of Black children being protected by soldiers as they tried to go to school. Jim wrote articles about these events, which were published in the *Chicago Defender*.

The struggle for voting rights and the end of segregation was spreading throughout the South. Jim helped organize a support network in Chicago. Food, clothing and money were collected and sent to the people in Fayette County, Mississippi, who were struggling for their right to vote.

In 1961, some college students in the South came together to form the Student Nonviolent Coordinating Committee (SNCC, pronounced "snick"). Jim accepted an invitation to join them. He moved to Atlanta and was elected Executive Secretary of SNCC. Now he could fulfill his lifelong dream of helping people gain their freedom.

The students in SNCC were very bold and their actions gained the attention of the whole world. One of the things they did was start Freedom Schools. These schools were modeled after those started by Septima Clark and the Highlander Center. Black people learned to read and write, and learned about their voting rights in the Freedom Schools.

While Jim worked with SNCC, he traveled in Europe and Africa telling people about racism in the United States and what SNCC was doing to end it. In Zambia, East Africa, Jim represented SNCC at a United Nations meeting on apartheid in South Africa. He also visited with Josephine Baker in Paris. Jim wrote articles about his meetings and sent them back to the United States.

W

Many thousands of Black and white people demonstrated in the South between 1961 and 1964. They often sang as they marched. Thousands of them were arrested and went to jail just for demonstrating and singing. Some people were even killed. But eventually their actions led to the passage of the 1964 Civil Rights Act, which made all segregation and discrimination illegal in the United States. This law was made stronger the following year by the 1965 Voting Rights Act.

Today James Forman lives in Washington, D.C. The citizens of the capital of the United States, most of whom are Black, still do not have their full voting rights. Although they elect representatives to Congress, those representatives cannot vote. James Forman is working to change the law so that the District of Columbia will be made into a state to be known as "New Columbia."

*Andy wanted all nations
to work out their differences peacefully.*

*"If we understand our differences,
maybe we can solve our problems."*

ANDREW YOUNG

1932 – present

Andy was so angry he was about to turn purple! One of the new kids in the neighborhood had called him a bad name. As he got ready to punch the other kid in the face, Andy remembered his father's words:

"Don't get mad, get smart!"

Andy backed away from the other boy. He thought, "Hitting this guy won't change the fact that he called me a bad name." The boy was waiting for Andy to start a fight. Now he stared at him.

"What's wrong?" he said.

"If I hit you, will you stop calling Black people bad names?" asked Andy. After thinking a minute, the boy said, "Probably not."

Remembering the black eye he had gotten in a fight the past week, Andy put his fists down. "I'd rather talk to you than fight," he said. "Why did you call me that name, anyway?"

This was the beginning of Andrew Young's career as a peacemaker.

Andrew Young was born and raised in New Orleans, Louisiana. His father, Dr. Andrew Young, Sr., was a dentist. The Youngs lived in a white neighborhood and Andy and his younger brother Walter grew up playing with white kids. "The only racial disturbances on the block occurred when people from outside the neighbor-hood would come and see those two little black boys playing with a group of white boys," says Andy's mother. "We taught our boys that such people didn't know any better, that they were white people who were insecure about their own race."

But living in a white neighborhood did not mean that the Youngs could go places and do things alongside their neighbors. Andy and Walter went to a Black school. They could not visit libraries, play in parks or eat in restau-rants that were for whites only. As soon as Andy could talk, he started asking "Why? Why can't we go there?" It wasn't until he was a man that Andy began to answer this question for himself.

Andy was curious about everything and he loved to read. He got good grades in school, but he preferred playing sports and joking with his friends. He graduated from high school at fifteen, and at sixteen he enrolled at Howard University in Washington, D.C. He was much younger than his classmates, and most of the time he felt like a kid. He did well in his classes, but Andy was disappointed when he did not make the track or swim teams. He wanted to prove that he was a man, like his older classmates. In his senior year, Andy finally made both the track and swim teams.

Just before he graduated from college, Andy began to wonder if he had really learned anything in school. What was he going to do with his life? His parents wanted him to become a dentist. Andy did not want to do this, but he agreed to try. The summer before he was to start dental school, he met a white minister who was going to Africa.

This young missionary and Andy became friends. They talked long into the night about the problems facing Africans and African-Americans. Andy was impressed by this man who was willing to give up making money and getting ahead in order to help others. "He challenged my whole concept of manhood," Andy recalls. "Maybe it wasn't about being on a swim team or making money."

After spending a summer at a Christian camp, Andy decided to become a minister. He enrolled at Hartford Theological Seminary in Connecticut when he was nineteen. For the first time, he was interested in school. He learned how people had solved problems peacefully in the past. He especially liked the teachings of Mohandas Gandhi, who led the people of India in a nonviolent movement to get the British out of India. Andy remembered his father's saying, "Don't get mad, get smart."

After Andy graduated, he became pastor of a tiny, whitewashed church that served two towns in Georgia, Thomasville and Beachton. Looking out at his congregation made him sad. Here were African-American people who worked the rich soil of Georgia, but couldn't own the farms they labored on. White people had told them they would lose their homes if they tried to vote to change things. Andy told the people, "Don't be afraid, get out there and vote. It's the only way we're going to change anything! I'll stand with you!"

As Andy was working with his community, another young minister named Martin Luther King, Jr. was also encouraging people to get out and vote. Andy and Martin met and became good friends. They decided to work together in the Civil Rights Movement to bring about change.

Andy began directing a voter's registration drive in Albany, Georgia. He became a powerful leader and organizer, planning marches. He worked with Martin Luther King in the Southern Christian Leadership Conference until Dr. King was killed.

After Martin Luther King's assassination, Andy wondered what he should do. He wanted to work for change in a different way. He decided to run for Congress. Then he would have a say in the shaping of the laws of the country. Andy lost the election the first time he ran, but he didn't give up. He tried again in 1972 and won. It was the same year that Barbara Jordon was elected to Congress in Texas.

As a congressman, Andy earned a reputation as a peacemaker. If two representatives were arguing, they would ask Andy to act as referee. President Jimmy Carter recognized Andy's peacemaking abilities and asked him to be the United States Ambassador to the United Nations. This was the highest government position ever held by an African-American at that time. Andy wanted all nations to work out their differences peacefully. "If we understand our differences, maybe we can solve our problems," said Andy.

After he had been ambassador for two years, Andrew Young was forced to step down from his position. Andrew always said what he thought, even if it was not popular, and some American politicians did not like this. Andy's opinions and his peacemaking efforts cost him his job, but it was not long before he found other work. In 1982, Andrew Young was elected mayor of Atlanta, Georgia. He still believed in creating jobs for people and making sure everyone had the opportunity to receive a good education.

"The struggle that began with the Civil Rights movement continues today. We must all get together peacefully to change what is unfair. Let's all get smart instead of getting mad."

*Barbara Jordan was the first African-American elected
to the Texas State Senate in over thirty years.*

BARBARA JORDAN

1936 - present

"Barbara, Barbara." The crowd shouted her name over and over again. Barbara Jordan stood on the steps of the Texas State capitol gazing out at the thousands of people gathered there. They had come to celebrate Barbara Jordan Day. She was the first African-American to be chosen governor for the day. She was a tall, chocolate-colored woman wearing sturdy black-framed glasses. But behind that serious gaze was a knowing smile. Looking out at the people, she recalled when she was a little girl.

•••••

"Grandpa, where are we going today?" young Barbara asked.

"Over to the other side of Houston today, baby girl." Grandfather Patten collected junk, the things no one wanted any more. Little brown-eyed Barbara was his faithful assistant.

"Got your old clothes on?" Grandpa would ask Barbara. "Don't want you getting your good clothes dirty." After Grandpa hitched up the wagon he handed Barbara the reins for the mules and off they went.

Barbara was Grandpa's scout looking for good junk. "Look Grandpa," she would squeal, "there are some treasures!" Grandpa would pull the wagon over and get down to see if the stuff was good. They would put it in the wagon to sell later. Barbara sat up straight on the wagon seat, proud of being a good scout.

"You're an extraordinary person, Barbara.
You're going to do great things."

Barbara and Grandpa often talked as they worked. "You're an *extraordinary* person, Barbara. You're going to do great things. Just listen to your Grandpa, I've seen a lot and I can tell," Grandpa Patten would say. Barbara believed him. She knew he'd lived a hard life. He had even spent time in jail for a crime he had not committed. He never attended a school with white children or lived in a neighborhood with people of different races.

After these important conversations with her grandpa, Barbara would square her skinny shoulders, retie the red ribbons on the ends of her braids and whisper to herself, "I will live an *extraordinary* life." Grandpa trusted Barbara so much that he had her keep track of the money for his business. He gave her a money belt that fit snugly around her waist, under her coveralls. Barbara kept very accurate accounts of all the money.

• • • • •

"Mama, please pass me the sweet potato pie," said Barbara. Her mother sliced a fluffy, pumpkin-colored piece and slid it onto a plate.

"Barbara, I'm so proud of you. Imagine our baby girl being the first girl chosen to represent our state in a speech contest," said Mrs. Jordan.

Barbara smiled. She felt proud, and was determined that this was just the beginning. She had decided that she would be a very good student when she started school. She read every book she could get her hands on. "I will live an *extraordinary* life," Barbara still whispered to herself. It took lots of study to be outstanding, but it was worth it. Barbara smiled as she ate the last of her mother's luscious pie.

Houston was still a very segregated city when Barbara was a student. Black people lived on one side of town and whites on the other. They never came together to visit or play. "Why does it have to be like this?" she asked. The grownups simply said, "Because it's always been that way."

This answer bothered Barbara very much. She knew that because of the color of her skin, she could only attend all-Black schools and colleges. There wasn't anything wrong with African-American schools, she just wanted to meet other people.

While she was in high school, Barbara decided to become a lawyer. She saw that making new laws was a good way to end segregation. She would work to make it illegal to keep people separated because of their skin color. In 1956, after graduating from college, Barbara was accepted to the Boston University Law School. Three years later she graduated with honors.

Barbara returned to Texas and set up a law practice. She couldn't afford to rent an office so she worked with her clients at her parent's dining room table. She practiced many different kinds of law. Adoption was Barbara's favorite type of case to work on.

In 1960, Barbara volunteered to work on John Kennedy's presidential campaign. At first, she stuffed envelopes and ran the copy machine. Soon she was making speeches. When Barbara spoke, people listened. When she was asked to run for public office herself, she ran for the Texas State Senate. The first two times she ran, she lost. But Barbara Jordan was not a quitter. In 1966, she was elected to the Texas Senate. She was the first African-American elected to the state senate in over 30 years.

In 1972, Barbara Jordan ran for an even higher office, the United States House of Representatives. She won that election, too. She served for three terms, proving herself to be an *extraordinary* representative. Barbara was advisor to the judiciary committee at the impeachment hearings of President Richard Nixon.

In 1976, the Democratic National Committee asked her to be keynote speaker at their convention, the first African-American to have this honor. Her speech was so good people wanted her to run for president of the United States!

In 1979, Barbara decided to retire from public office and look for a new kind of challenge. She accepted a professorship at the Lyndon B. Johnson School of Public Affairs at the University of Texas at Austin. There she teaches students about history and how to be part of the political process.

Grandpa Patten was right. With her many accomplishments, Barbara Jordan is indeed an *extraordinary* person.

Adult

Baker, Josephine, and Joe Bouillon. *Josephine.* New York, New York: Harper & Row Publishers, Inc.,1977.

Brooks, Gwendolyn. *A Street in Bronzeville.* New York, New York: Harper and Brothers, 1945.

Brooks, Gwendolyn. *Report From Part One: An Autobiography.* Detroit, Michigan: Broadside Press, 1972.

Brooks, Gwendolyn. *Beckonings.* Detroit, Michigan: Broadside Press, 1975.

Brooks, Gwendolyn. *A Capsule Course in Black Poetry Writing.* Detroit, Michigan: Broadside Press, 1975.

Forman, James. *The Making of Black Revolutionaries.* Washington, D.C.: Open Hand Publishing, 1985.

Gardner, Carl. *Andrew Young: A Biography.* New York, New York: Drake Publishers Inc., 1978.

Haskins, James. *Barbara Jordon.* New York, New York: The Dial Press, 1977.

Haskins, James. *Andrew Young: Man With A Mission.* New York, New York: Lothrop, Lee & Shepard Company, 1979.

Jordon, Barbara & Hearon, Shelby. *Barbara Jordon: A Self-Portrait.* Garden City, New York: Doubleday Company, Inc., 1979.

Melhem, D. H. *Gwendolyn Brooks: Poetry and the Heroic Voice.* Lexington, Kentucky: The University of Kentucky Press, 1987.

Rose, Phyllis. *Jazz Cleopatra: Josephine Baker In Her Time.* New York, New York: Doubleday, 1989.

Children

Aldred, Lisa. *Thurgood Marshall: Supreme Court Justice.* New York, New York: Chelsea House, 1990.

Brooks, Gwendolyn. *Bronzeville Boys and Girls.* New York, New York: Harper & Row, Publishers Inc., 1965.

Fenderson, Lewis H. *Thurgood Marshall, Fighter for Justice.* New York, New York: McGraw Hill Book Company, 1969.

Hammond, Bryan and Patrick O'Conner, *Josephine Baker.* Boston, Massachusetts: Little Brown, 1991.

Roberts, Maurice. *Andrew Young, Freedom Fighter.* Chicago, Illinois: Children's Press, 1983.

Roberts, Maurice. *Barbara Jordon: The Great Lady From Texas.* Chicago, Illinois: Children's Press, 1983.

Simpson, Jan. *Andrew Young, A Matter of Choice.* St. Paul, Minnesota: EMC Corporation, 1978.

Westman, Paul. *Andrew Young, Champion of the Poor.* Minneapolis, Minnesota: Dillon Press, Inc., 1983.

Young, Margaret. *The Picture Life of Thurgood Marshall.* New York, New York: Franklin Walts, Inc., 1971.